About the Editor

Rebecca Raffaelli is on the faculty of Neighborhood Music School in New Haven, Connecticut, where she serves as adult program coordinator. She received both her BM and MM degrees from Boston University, where her teachers included Esther Mills Wood, Leonard Shure, and Russell Sherman. An active performer, teacher, and adjudicator, Ms. Raffaelli has performed solo and chamber music in the United States and Europe, and has a large private studio. She has recorded the *Sonata, Opus 25* and the *Nocturne, Opus 32, No. 1* by Dianne Goolkasian Rahbee. Ms. Raffaelli has also taught at Wesleyan University.

Series Editor

Helen Marlais has given collaborative recitals throughout the U.S. and in Canada, Italy, France, Germany, Turkey, Hungary, Lithuania, Russia, and China. She is recorded on Gasparo and Centaur record labels, and has performed and given workshops at local, state and national music teachers' conventions, including the National Conference on Keyboard Pedagogy and the National Music Teacher's convention. She is Director of Keyboard Publications for The FJH Music Company and her articles can be read in major keyboard journals.

Dr. Marlais is an associate professor of piano at Grand Valley State University in Grand Rapids, MI. She has also held full-time faculty piano positions at the Crane School of Music, S.U.N.Y. at Potsdam, Iowa State University, and Gustavus Adolphus College.

Volume 1
Table of Contents

Early Intermediate through Late Intermediate

The Preludes can be performed individually or in any groupings the performer wishes.

Volume 2
Table of Contents

Late Intermediate through Advanced

This is a favorite piece of the composer's. It expresses the physical and emotional fragility
of aging. It also has two distinct different ways of being perceived. The piece features a
pedal point figure of a single repeated note that depicts iron bars like those in a jail cell.
The performer may choose to be inside the cell looking out at life, or outside the cell
looking in at the prisoner. This extremely sensitive piece requires *pianissimo* control.

"Intchu" is the Armenian word for "why." The piece is an emotional lament over the
suffering of the Armenian people, past and present.

A playful pianistic experience featuring fourths.

A very slow and serious contemplative piece; to be played with calm resignation.

This piece expresses defiance and resolve to overcome all odds!

This is a happy and playful, free-spirited piece.

Inspired by the humorous spirit of great Hungarian composer, Gyorgy Ligeti.

The Preludes can be performed individually or in any groupings the performer wishes.

Volumes 1 and 2
Preludes by Opus number

Early Intermediate through Advanced

for Edward (Ted) Hennessy (1966-2001)

Prelude
In Memoriam
Op. 116

Dianne Goolkasian Rahbee
2001

With feelings of anguish after the World Trade Center disaster on 9/11/01.

Molto espressivo (♩ = ca. 92)

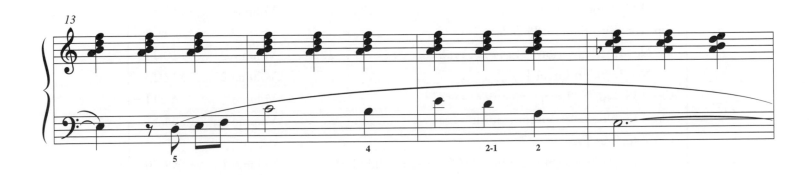

* Bring out bottom voice of the *R.H.* chords.
** Bring out top notes of *R.H.* chords.

Prelude

Op. 4, No. 8

Dianne Goolkasian Rahbee

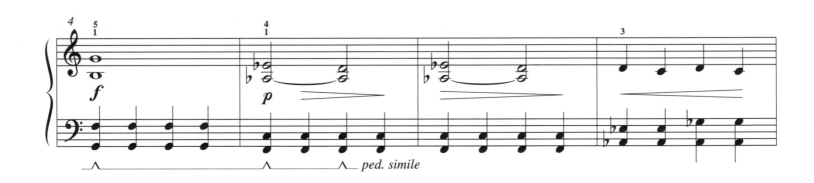

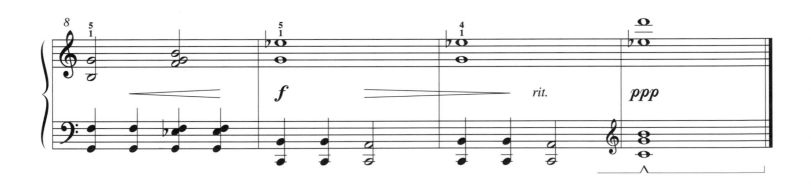

for Mildred Freiberg

Prelude

Escape to Inner Space

Op. 138, No. 1

Sans rigueur; in a slow, relaxed manner
To be played very freely, as if improvising.

Dianne Goolkasian Rahbee
2004

Repeat ad lib. as many times as you wish, each time improvising rhythmically and dynamically using the given notes.

J1017

Prelude

Op. 4, No. 4

Dianne Goolkasian Rahbee

Restful and expressive (♩ = 76)

12

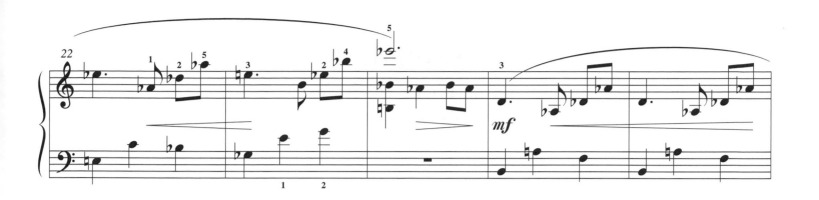

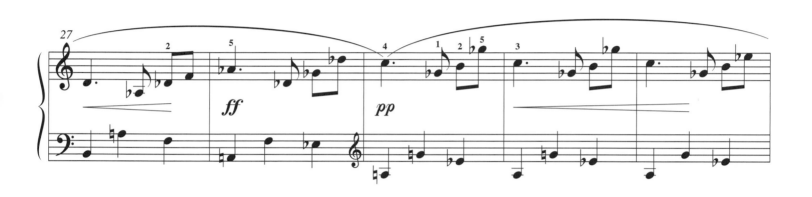

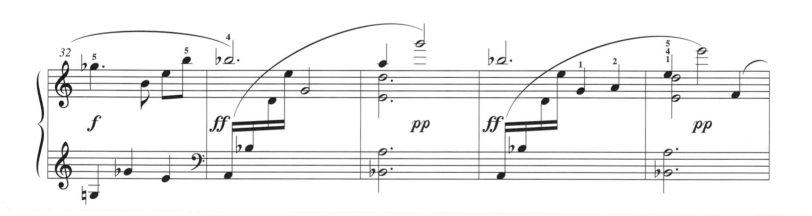

for Sylvia Griffith

Prelude
from *Three Preludes*
Op. 5, No. 1

Dianne Goolkasian Rahbee

Espressivo (♩ = 80 or faster)

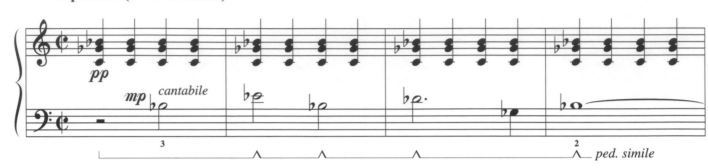

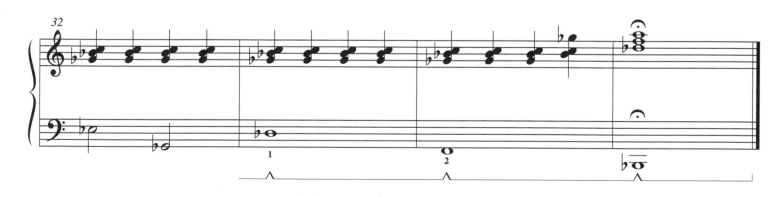

for Marjorie Burgess

Prelude

from *Three Preludes*

Op. 5, No. 2

Dianne Goolkasian Rahbee

Moderato espressivo ($\quarternote = 60$)

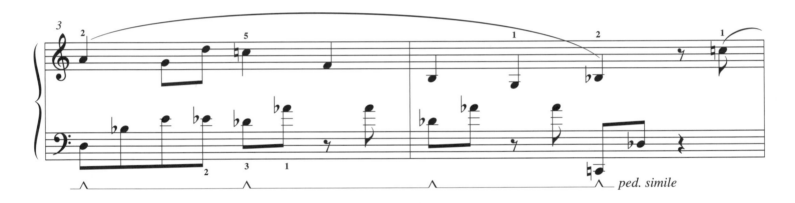

for *Alberto Ginastera*

Prelude

from *Three Preludes*

Op. 5, No. 3

Dianne Goolkasian Rahbee

* *L.H.* may be *legato* or *non-legato.*

Prelude
Op. 46

Dianne Goolkasian Rahbee
1991

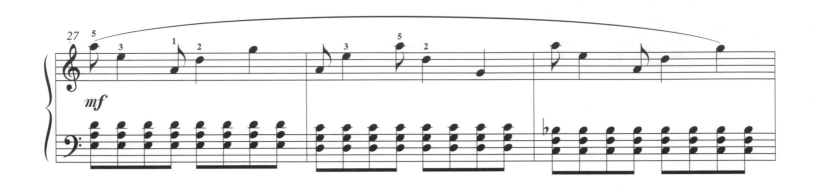

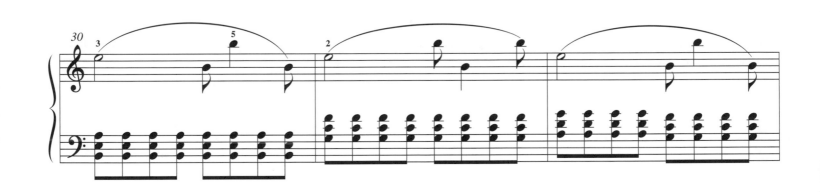

for Mariann Abraham

Prelude

August, from *Three Preludes*

Op. 87, No. 1

Dianne Goolkasian Rahbee
1998

Restlessly (♩ = 120)

* Bring out: e.v.; t.v.; m.v.; b.v. (equal, top, middle, or bottom voice).

N.B. The performer should use discretion in pedaling whenever a specific pedal is not marked.

J1017

26

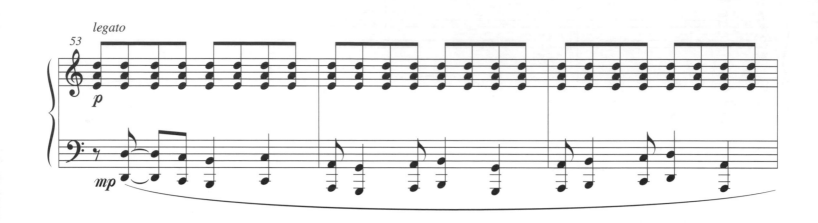

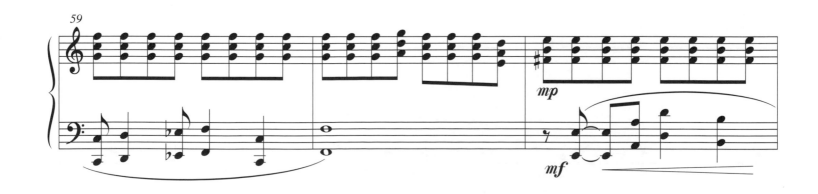

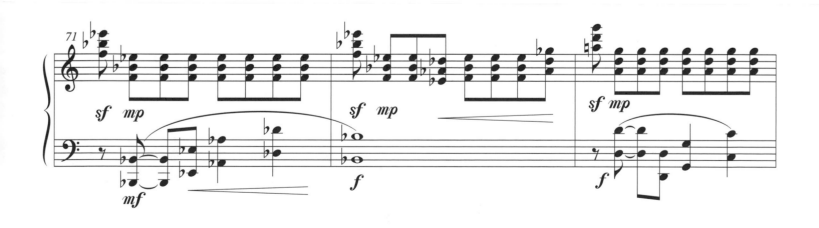

for Mariann Abraham

Prelude

Lullaby for Elias, from *Three Preludes*

Op. 87, No. 2

Dianne Goolkasian Rahbee
1998

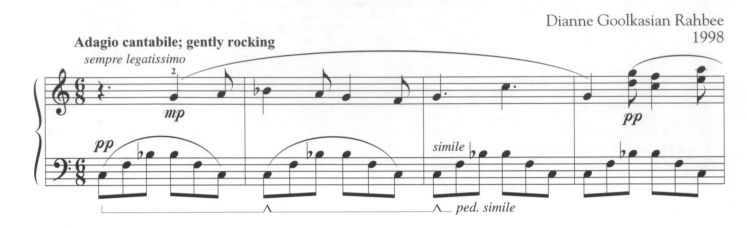

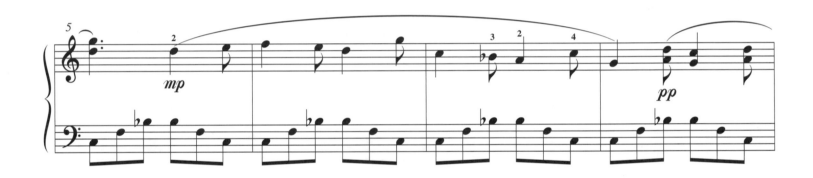

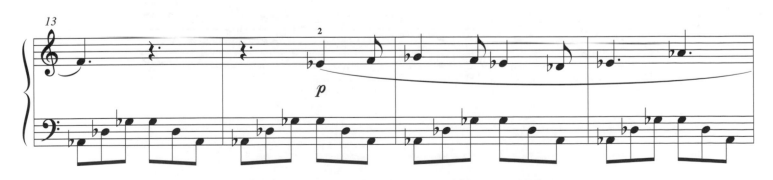

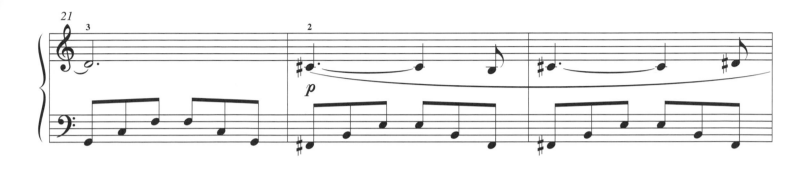

*Repeat is not necessary *(ad lib).*

for Mariann Abraham

Prelude

Celebration, from *Three Preludes*

Op. 87, No. 3

Dianne Goolkasian Rahbee
1998

Allegretto, molto energico (♩ = 168)

for Dad's 88th Birthday

Prelude
Melody
Op. 88

Dianne Goolkasian Rahbee
1998

Andante cantabile (♪ = 136)

molto espressivo e rubato

mp

ped. simile

p

mp

8va - - - - - -

mp

* t.v.
b.v.

p

* Bring out: e.v.; t.v.; m.v.; b.v. (equal, top, middle, or bottom voice).

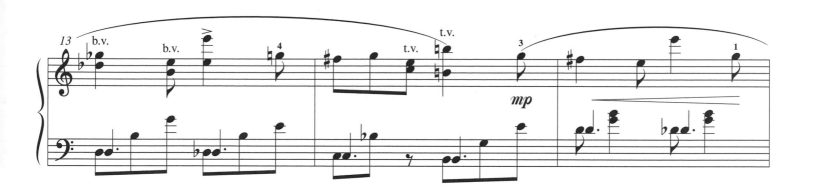

Prelude
Chaotic Life in the 90's
Op. 90

Dianne Goolkasian Rahbee
1998

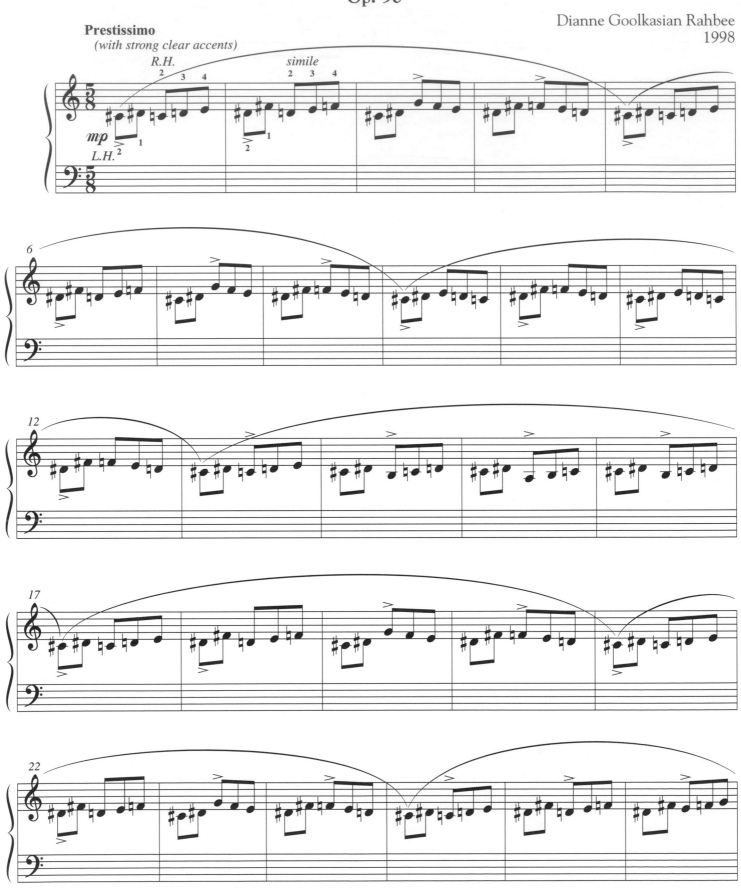

Time to stop and smell the roses!   FOR WHOM THE BELLS TOLL!

* Arm clusters are to be played using the right arm from the wrist to the elbow on the black keys below Middle C, and using the left arm from the elbow to the wrist on the white keys below Middle C. Drop both arms on the keys, rolling from left to right, as if in total exhaustion. Keep head down low as cluster fades away.

for Inge Holleck

Prelude

Moving Along

Op. 115, No. 2

Dianne Goolkasian Rahbee
2001

Allegretto

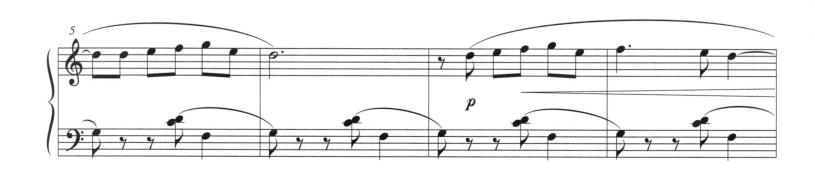

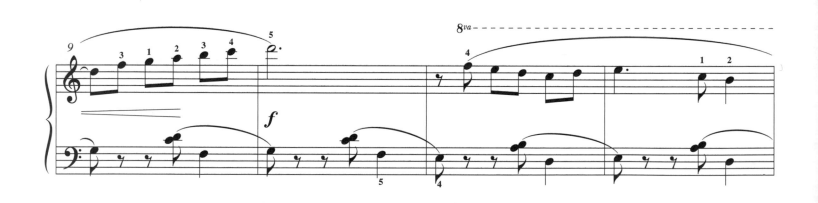

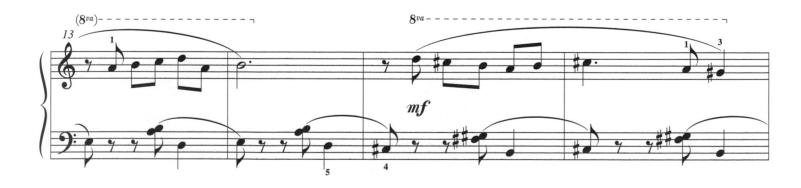

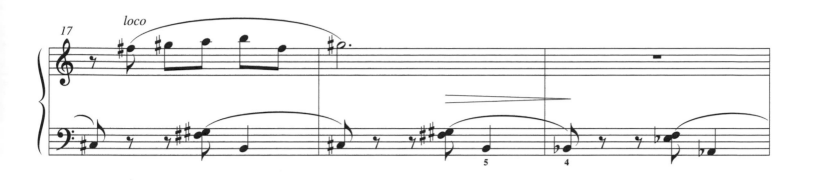

for Inge Holleck

Prelude
Searching for Answers
Op. 115, No. 1

Dianne Goolkasian Rahbee
2001

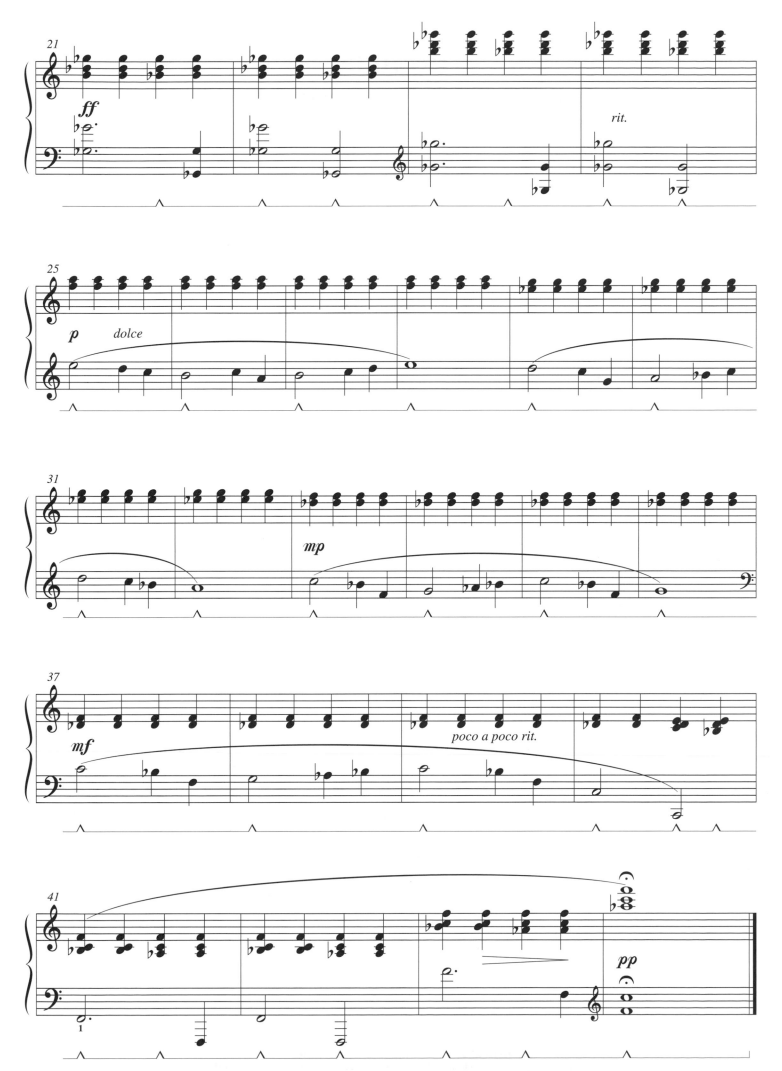

for Inge Holleck

Prelude
A Garden of Fragile Flowers with Deep Roots
Op. 115, No. 3

Dianne Goolkasian Rahbee
2001

Espressivo, ad libitum (♩ = 48-76)
from delicate fragile textures to deep roots of strength

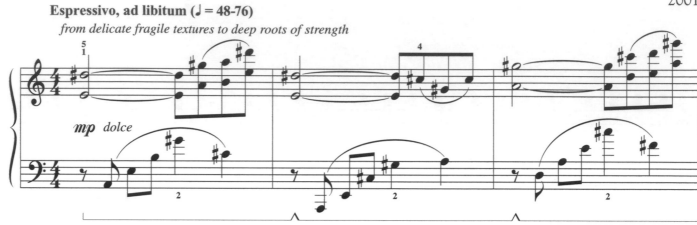

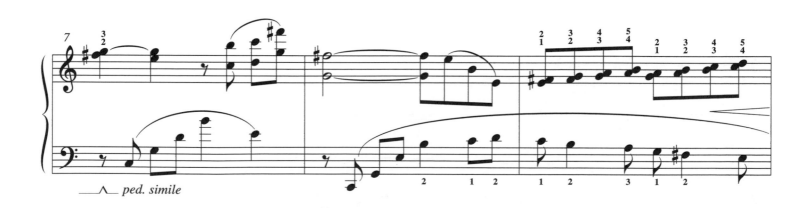

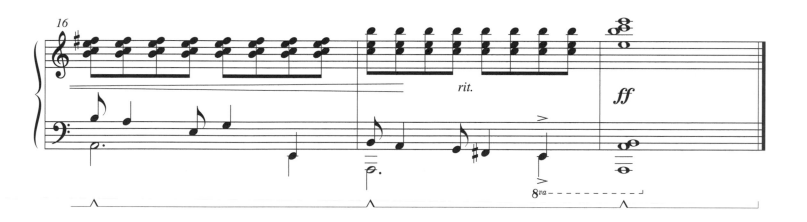

Prelude
Autumn
Op. 89

Dianne Goolkasian Rahbee
1998

The top notes of all R.H. chords must sing out

Dolente (♩ = 69)

Molto espressivo

cantabile e dolce

Sing out with a rich deep tone quality

* Bring out: e.v.; t.v.; m.v.; b.v. (equal, top, middle, or bottom voice).

Bring out all top R.H. notes

pp

poco a poco cresc. to the end

ped. simile

for Elizabeth Orens

Prelude

Dialogue, from *Three Preludes*

Op. 18, No. 7

Dianne Goolkasian Rahbee

for John Heiss

Prelude

Flute Frolic, from *Three Preludes*

Op. 18, No. 1

Dianne Goolkasian Rahbee
1983

J1017

(a) Trill the entire measure starting on the main note.

Prelude
Capriccio, from *Three Preludes*
Op. 18, No. 5

Dianne Goolkasian Rahbee

With energy (♪ = 184 or faster)

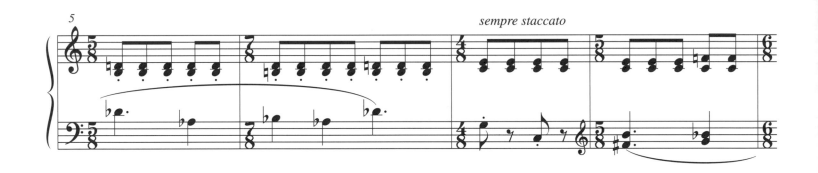

sempre staccato

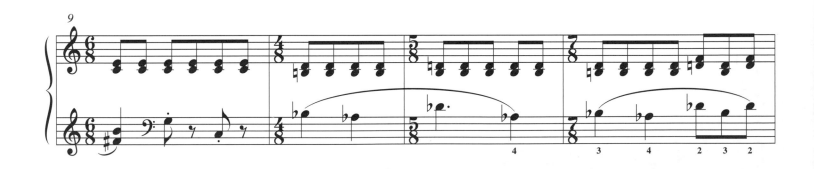

Prelude

Whim

Op. 62

Dianne Goolkasian Rahbee
1994

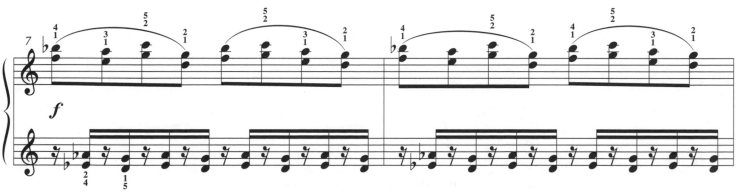